WATKINS & MILLER HALLS

University of Kansas

Compiled by Norma Decker Hoagland
Designed by Shala Stevenson

Historic Mount Oread Friends
Lawrence, Kansas

This book was made possible by the generous donations of members of Kitchen 8, the alumnae organization for Watkins and Miller Scholarship Halls at KU. For more information about Kitchen 8 activities, newsletters, and events go to www.kitchen8.org.

WATKINS AND MILLER HALLS
is published by Historic Mount Oread Friends
Kansas University Endowment Association
University of Kansas
Lawrence, Kansas 66045 USA

 First edition 2016

Printed in the United States of America
Distributed by the University Press of Kansas

Library of Congress Control Number: 2015043773

Cover photo: Norma Decker Hoagland
Cover design: Shala Stevenson
Endsheets: First City Photo, Leavenworth, Kansas

The next time someone asks where you lived in college — you just tell them you lived in a Neoclassical "national landmark" with fluted Ionic columns that's on the National Register of Historic Places. In other words, you will tell them that you lived in a place that has stood the test of time.

It's the truth. You can say all that and more because on January 8, 2014, Watkins and Miller Halls finally earned their rightful place in history when the National Park Service (NPS) approved the Kansas Historical Society's (KHS) recommendation to put the Lilac Lane halls on the National Register.

[As another alumna said], "The halls are rich with historic significance. Watkins and Miller were the unique first-in-the-nation dream of Mrs. Watkins that made it possible for so many daughters of The Great Depression to get an education."

More than half of the 15 "contributing resources" in the East Historic District are scholarship halls, led by Watkins and Miller Halls, Elizabeth Miller Watkins's far-sighted experiment to "help the girls who must travel uphill."

"Elizabeth Miller Watkins is the lynchpin of the East Historic District," said **Sarah Jackson Martin** (Miller, 1998–2000), the National Register Coordinator with the Kansas Historical Society. "Her roots are in this district. She is the thread that connects most of the contributing resources in the East Historic District." . . . Mrs. Watkins funded or built and donated to KU almost every building on Lilac Lane.

— **Sarah Wohlrabe Shortall,** Watkins Hall, 1972–76, *Kitchen 8 Newsletter*, April 2014, pp. 1, 7

Elizabeth Josephine Miller was born in 1861 in New Paris, Ohio, and moved to Lawrence, Kansas, with her family when she was eleven. Her family included Valentine, her father, who was a physician; Ella, her mother; and brothers Frank and Edward. Dr. Miller had been a surgeon in the Union Army in the Civil War and was not in good health. Because of this, Elizabeth left school at fifteen and went to work as a secretary for Jabez B. Watkins, a land broker and mortgage banker. Her work changed her life. Her family's financial problems had kept her from earning a college degree, but these problems made her determined to help needy young women earn their KU diplomas.

Jabez had come to Lawrence from the East about the same time as the Millers. His decision to settle in Lawrence was pivotal to his future as well as to the future of Elizabeth, the city, and the University of Kansas. He was a savvy entrepreneur and became a millionaire. Elizabeth was J.B.'s astute student. They shared ideas for distributing his wealth. In 1909 J.B. and Elizabeth married. They soon built the Outlook, their home on Mount Oread, southeast of the KU campus, which is now the chancellor's residence. This five-acre site was also the future location of Watkins and Miller Halls.

JB continued to invest in land in Louisiana and western Kansas. He made arrangements for Elizabeth to own the Outlook and provided for her living expenses. He died in 1921. Elizabeth spent the next five years settling his estate.

In late 1925 she began to bring their plans to fruition. She and J.B. had wanted to benefit as many people as possible, especially young people. Because much of his estate was tied up in land holdings, she liquidated some assets to have ready cash.

Her first big project was Watkins Hall. At the time, there were several cooperative living groups serving KU students. But she took co-op living to a different level, and she wanted it to be for girls. She believed that it was important for its residents not only to get an academic education but also to learn useful skills: organization, academic excellence, bookkeeping, etiquette, household management, and cooking. These goals formed her vision for Watkins and Miller Halls.

She oversaw the business of the estate, land holdings in Louisiana and western Kansas, managed her household, and traveled. She also helped fund and plan the Lawrence Hospital, the KU hospital, and nurses' home. J.B. had taught her to be a "hands-on" manager. She was heavily involved in these projects until her death in 1939. Elizabeth Miller Watkins left the bulk of her fortune, mostly western Kansas land holdings, to the University of Kansas Endowment. Her many gifts continue to benefit KU students, Lawrence, and the University of Kansas.

— **Mary Burchill,** Elizabeth Miller Watkins' biographer

J.B. Watkins as a young man

Watkins Land Mortgage Company and Watkins National Bank, now the Watkins Museum of History

She went to work in the office of Mr. Watkins and became assistant secretary of the company . . . "Mr. Watkins recognized in her a woman of great ability," said W.O. Simons, editor and publisher of the Lawrence Journal World, who knew them both years ago when their business was active. "She helped him build up his fortune."

— *Kansas City Star,* February 24, 1935

. . . I do hereby assign, transfer and set over unto Miss Lizzie J. Miller the above-named Policy of Insurance, and all sum or sums of money, interest, benefit and advantage whatsoever . . . unto the said Miss Lizzie J. Miller during her life time, . . . the consideration for this assignment is no other than love and affection . . .

— Jabez B. Watkins, life insurance policy, December 14, 1900, Kitchen 8 Archives

The report reached Lawrence today from New York city, of the marriage there last week of Miss Lizzie Miller and Mr. J.B. Watkins, both of this city. It is not known when Mr. and Mrs. Watkins will return to Lawrence, where they will make their home. This announcement will be the most startling that has been made in several years, for no one in Lawrence had any idea that the wedding was to take place. Mrs. Watkins has a large number of friends in this city where she has lived for many years. Mr. Watkins is considered one of the richest men in the West. He is president of Watkins bank of this city and president of the Watkins Land and Mortgage company beside other distinctive offices which he holds.

— *Lawrence Daily Journal,* November 15, 1909

Her large home, which overlooked the Wakarusa valley, was called "The Outlook." Frequently she spent her time on the sun porch watching and waving to the many students who passed by on their way to classes. She was fond of them and often commented that "we get such fine students."

— *Lawrence Journal World*, June 1, 1939

After their marriage in 1909, when J.B. was sixty-four and Elizabeth was forty-eight, they built their Neo-Classical Revival-style home on land purchased from Kansas Governor Charles Robinson. Jabez lived there until his death in 1921 and Elizabeth gave the Outlook to KU as the chancellor's residence on her passing in 1939.

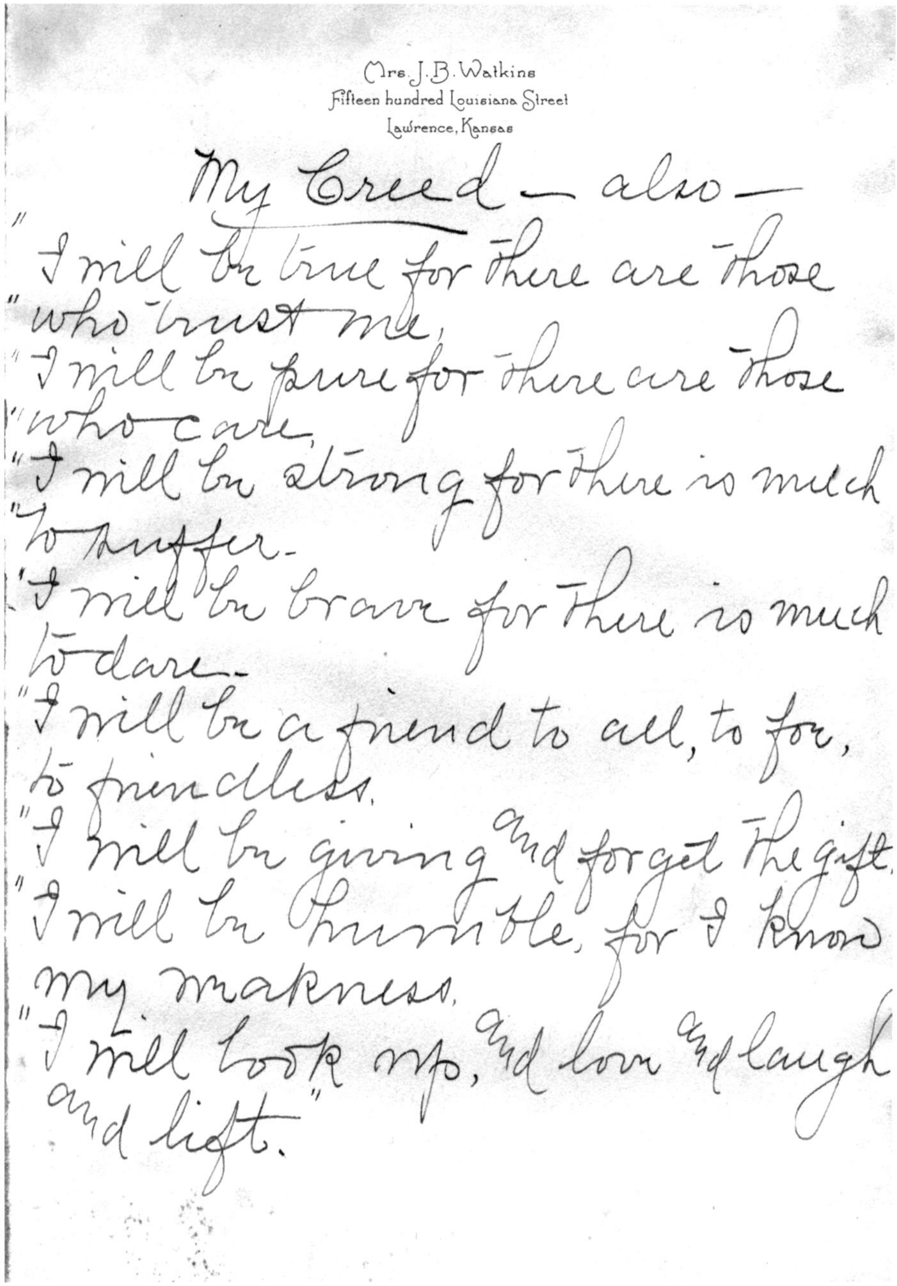

Mrs. J. B. Watkins
Fifteen hundred Louisiana Street
Lawrence, Kansas

My Creed — also —

"I will be true for there are those who trust me,
"I will be pure for there are those who care,
"I will be strong for there is much to suffer.
"I will be brave for there is much to dare.
"I will be a friend to all, to foe, to friendless.
"I will be giving and forget the gift.
"I will be humble, for I know my weakness.
"I will look up, and love and laugh and lift."

My Creed – *also* –

I will be true for there are those who trust me,
I will be pure for there are those who care.
I will be strong, for there is much to suffer,
I will be brave for there is much to dare.
I will be friend to all, to foe, to friendless,
I will be giving and forget the gift.
I will be humble, for I know my weakness.
I will look up, and love and laugh and lift.

She began her scrapbook four days after Franklin D. Roosevelt was inaugurated . . . The first page of the scrapbook is her creed, which is a Methodist hymn she entitles "My Creed, Also." . . . The members of Watkins Hall and Miller Hall follow this creed and recite it at an annual tribute night which remembers . . . how Mrs. Watkins contributed to their lives and to the many others throughout the community.

— **Sam Birchfield Bunnyfield,** Watkins Hall, 2003–07, "Elizabeth Miller Watkins: A Legacy Which Transcends Time," 2005, pp. 1–2, Kitchen 8 Archives

End to Lawrence Business Pioneer

J.B. Watkins died at his home here yesterday afternoon
Noted as a Builder
Since 1873 Had Figured as Financier, Railroad Builder and Land Owner
Helped to Develop Lake Charles, La., in Management of Land Project There

— *Lawrence Daily Journal-World* headline, February 5, 1921, p. 1

This photo of Elizabeth Watkins hangs in the Council Room of Watkins Scholarship Hall.

"And eventually you will give it all away?"

"Yes. We had no children and our plan was to give it all for the good of humanity, chiefly here in Lawrence, where the estate was brought together. We planned many things, but my husband died in 1921 before our plans were all made."

— **Elizabeth Miller Watkins,** interview by A.B. MacDonald, *Kansas City Star,* February 24, 1935

Chancellor E.H. Lindley said . . . "Mr. Watkins was a great generous-souled man. He helped hundreds of young men, especially students at this university. After his death Mrs. Watkins followed in the same path."

— *Kansas City Star,* February 24, 1935

My sympathy has always been with the girls who must travel up-hill. My husband and I had intended to do something that would really be beneficial to them. It has been my dream to aid self-supporting girls to get an education. I planned the hall so that the girls would have the advantages of life in a small group along with those enjoyed by a larger unit.

— **Elizabeth Miller Watkins,** *University Daily Kansan,* June 1, 1939

Thomas Williamson, of Topeka, has been chosen architect for the new dormitory for girls being built by Mrs. J. B. Watkins, of Lawrence. Mrs. Watkins will leave for Topeka tomorrow to complete plans for the new building. Goldwyn Goldsmith, professor of architecture, will accompany her and assist with the drawing of the plans. The new dormitory will be built opposite Fraser hall. It is to house women who are working their way through school.

— *University Daily Kansan,* September 22, 1925

One of Kansas' most prolific designers of public buildings during the first decades of the twentieth century, Thomas W. Williamson designed Topeka High School, Topeka, Kansas, and the Jayhawk Hotel, Theater and Walk, Topeka, Kansas, both listed on the National Historic Register. *He also designed Sumner Elementary School, Topeka, Kansas, a National Historic Landmark associated with the 1954 Supreme Court case* Brown v. Board of Education.

Two gifts of considerable size and of outstanding importance have come to the University recently. The first, a $50,000 hall of residence for women who are working their way through K.U., was announced July 1 as a gift from Mrs. J. B. Watkins of Lawrence. . . .

The house to be built by Mrs. Watkins will have rooms for forty girls or more and will be ready for occupancy by the opening of the fall term next year. It will stand on the north end of the Watkins property just east of Fraser hall. . . .

Mrs. Watkins and her late husband had long hoped for some means of assisting worthy students but had not been able to make plans for more than a few young people at a time. With the erection of this hall of residence it will be possible to provide lodging for a large number of University women at a nominal cost.

— *Graduate Magazine,* October 1925, p. 18

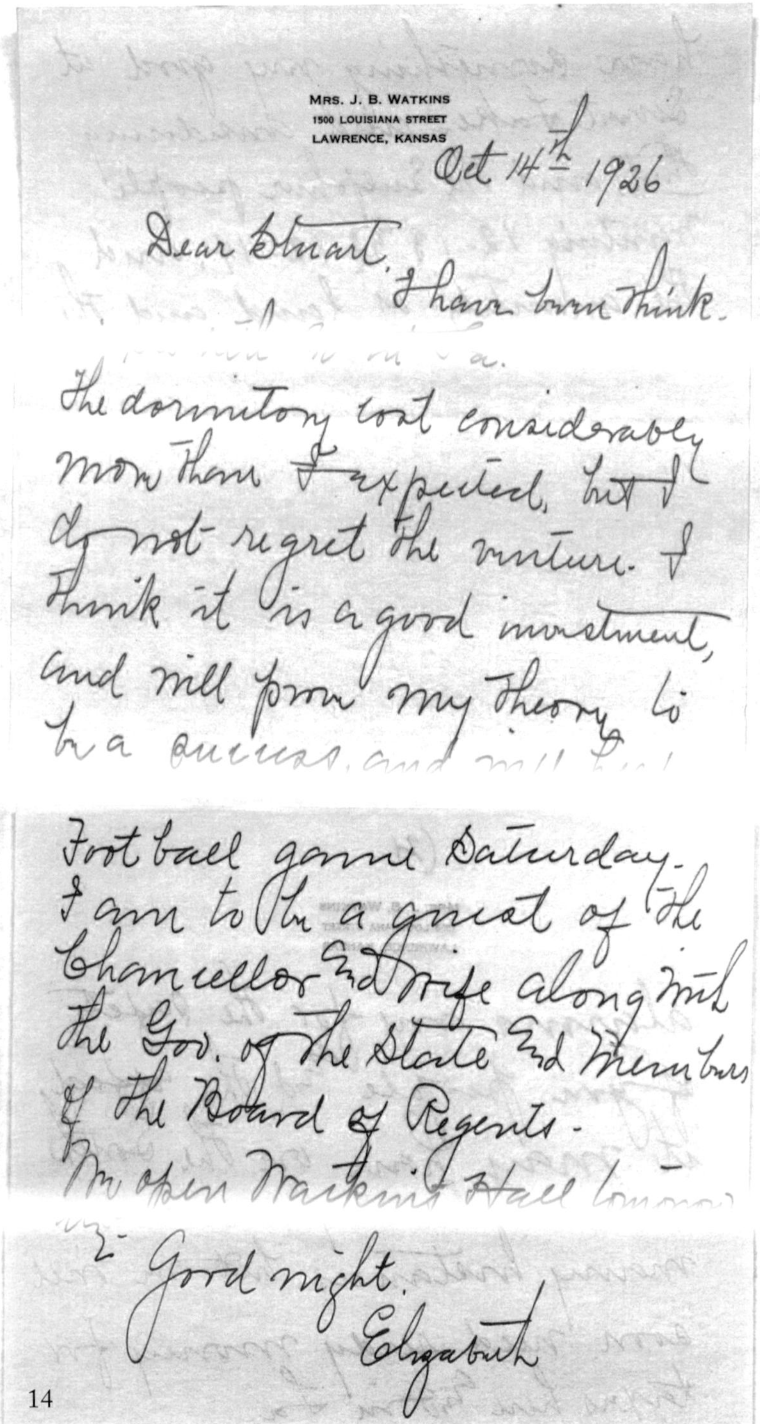

Mrs. J. B. Watkins
1500 Louisiana Street
Lawrence, Kansas

Oct 14th 1926

Dear Stuart,

I have been think-

The dormitory cost considerably more than I expected, but I do not regret the venture. I think it is a good investment, and will prove my theory to be a success,

Foot ball game Saturday. I am to be a guest of the Chancellor and wife along with the Gov. of the State and members of the Board of Regents. We open Watkins Hall tomorrow

Good night.
Elizabeth

Oct 14th 1926

Dear Stuart,

The dormitory cost considerably more than I expected, but I do not regret the venture. I think it is a good investment, and will prove my theory to be a success, and will help many students in the years to come to get an education and my future is largely behind me and I want to help humanity.

Good night,
Elizabeth

[Stuart Thomson was the Watkins' Louisiana property manager and an adviser for Elizabeth after Jabez's death.]

Oct 21st 1926

Dear Stuart,

Football game Saturday. I am to be a guest of the Chancellor and wife along with the Gov. of the State and members of the Board of Regents.

We open Watkins Hall tomorrow to the Public. The Chancellor and wife, the House President, the Chaperone, Dean of Women and your humble servant receive. The house is beautiful and as it was "Home Coming" day for the Alumni, the Chancellor thought it would be an opportune time to give our friends the chance to inspect, as so many are anxious to see it.

It seems to be a success in every way, and it is doing good beyond my expectations.

Yours truly,
Elizabeth M. Watkins

The official opening this afternoon of Watkins Hall, the new dormitory for self-supporting women, marks the beginning of a new era in the college life of working women of the University.

Through the generosity of Mrs. J.B. Watkins, donor of the building, the difficulties of securing an education have been made easier for a number of women.

Not only are the living conditions of Watkins hall a great improvement over those of other houses, but the amount of outside work necessary to make ends meet, is cut down considerably.

This means simply that students are enabled to go to school who otherwise could not, and that others are provided a means of continuing their education longer than would be possible under the circumstances. It means also a greater amount of time in which to study or take part in University activities.

Mrs. Watkins . . . did well to make as a requisite a high scholastic standing. The need of such a building on the campus is great, and the method of discriminating as to who shall be occupants of the hall has been well chosen.

— *University Daily Kansan,* October 22, 1926

The first dedication plaque arrived inscribed "In Memory of Jabez B. Hopkins." Imagine the flurry of correspondence this error began!

This first class of Watkins "Girls" (1926) gather around the Sohmer grand piano that Mrs. Watkins purchased for the hall.

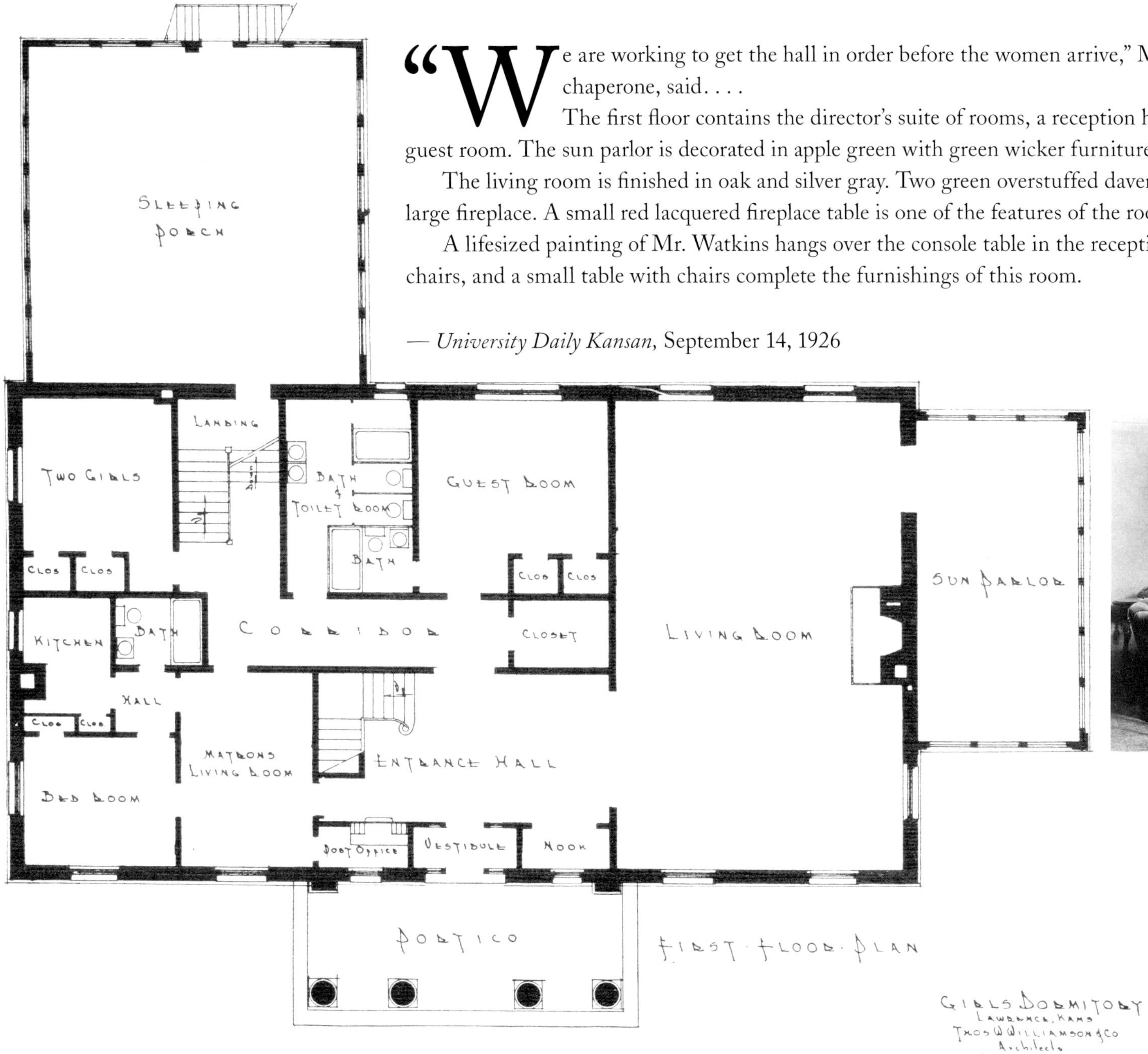

"We are working to get the hall in order before the women arrive," Mrs. R.C. Morrow, house chaperone, said. . . .

The first floor contains the director's suite of rooms, a reception hall, living room, sun parlor, and guest room. The sun parlor is decorated in apple green with green wicker furniture upholstered in pink and green.

The living room is finished in oak and silver gray. Two green overstuffed davenports are placed in front of the large fireplace. A small red lacquered fireplace table is one of the features of the room.

A lifesized painting of Mr. Watkins hangs over the console table in the reception hall. A desk, two tall backed chairs, and a small table with chairs complete the furnishings of this room.

— *University Daily Kansan,* September 14, 1926

"I have never done anything into which I have put more of myself," [**Elizabeth Watkins**] said. "The color scheme of every room, the furniture, draperies and furnishings are results of many months of planning. It is my dream come true."

— *University Daily Kansan,* June 1, 1939

Joyce Durall Redwine, 1948 graduate . . . remembered the strict house rules during her years. The women were not allowed to use the front hall, except for very special events, and men were allowed no further than the front lobby area.

— *University Daily Kansan,* October 13, 1986, p. 1

The rule for many years was that the front stairway, the formal stairs, was to be used "only on special occasions, when appropriately dressed."

Mrs. Watkins in her home, the Outlook

As **Katherine Monroe Cook,** 1933 graduate from Freemont, Ohio, toured Watkins, she remembered the kindness and generosity of Elizabeth Watkins . . .

[She] once took all of the women in the hall to a chicken dinner, Cook said, and then gave them each $10. To Cook, who was nearly broke at the time, it was very meaningful to receive the gift.

. . . "I feel that I'm part of something here bigger than myself," Cook said. "This was her dream, wasn't it?"

— *University Daily Kansan,* October 13, 1986, p. 1

Mary Ellen Roach Higgins (Watkins Hall 1938–42) recalls "meeting Mrs. Watkins twice, once in the entryway at Watkins Hall and being shown around her elegant home, now the chancellor's home, I believe. At Watkins she wore a dress of 1890's style, with standing collar."

— Alumnae Tea Memory Card, 2011, Kitchen 8 Archives

Elizabeth Watkins often visited Watkins Hall & I had the privilege of meeting her several times. She was a most gracious and caring person and always interested in the welfare of the students.

— **Frances Strait Brown,** Watkins Hall 1936–38, *Kitchen 8 Newsletter,* March 2011, p. 18

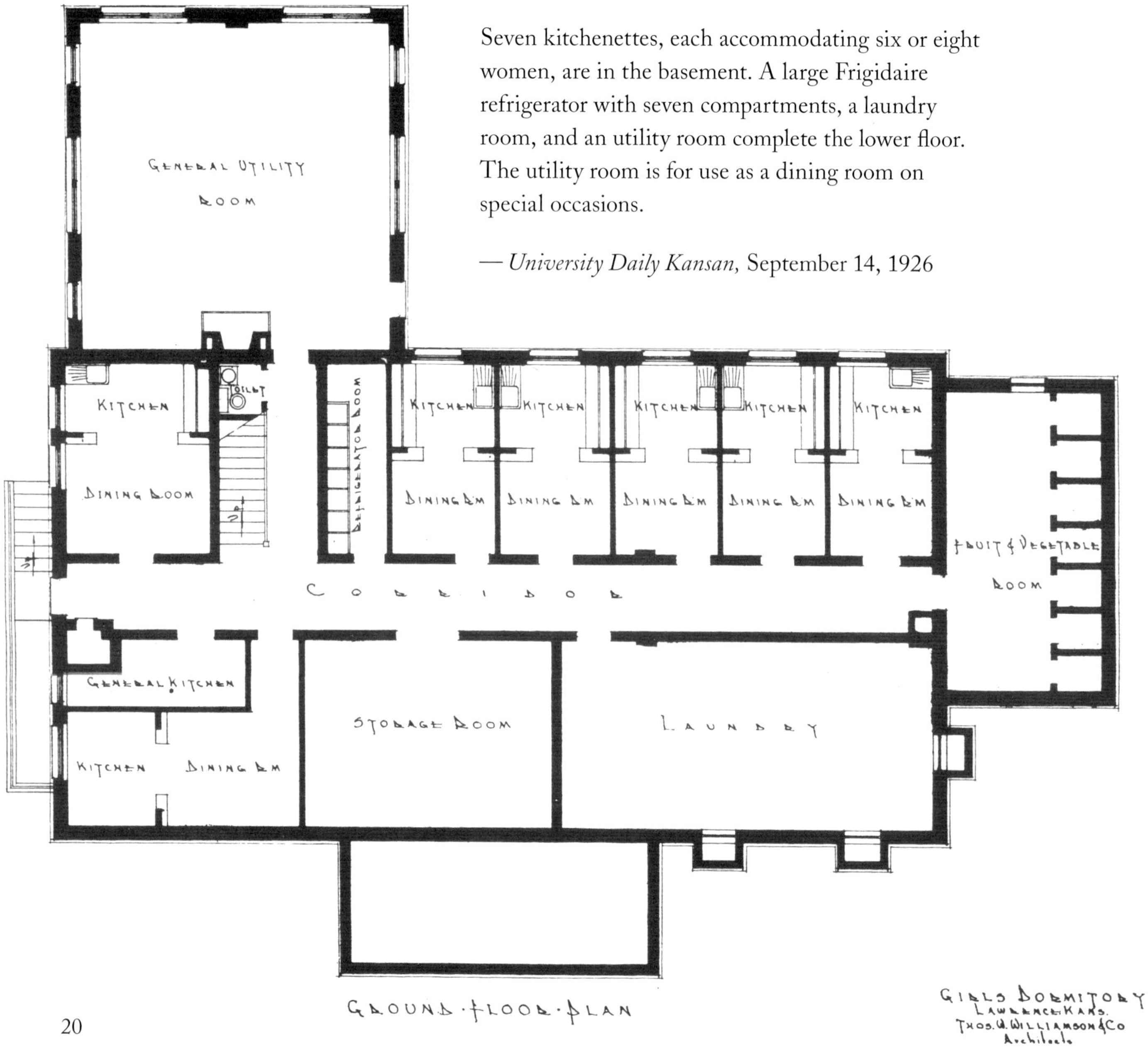

Seven kitchenettes, each accommodating six or eight women, are in the basement. A large Frigidaire refrigerator with seven compartments, a laundry room, and an utility room complete the lower floor. The utility room is for use as a dining room on special occasions.

— *University Daily Kansan,* September 14, 1926

KITCHEN NO. II

Alex: Clean dish cupboards, windows, stove, wastebasket.

Phil: Scrub floor on Wed. & Sat.; polish furniture.

Lucile: Upper cupboards, bread-box.

Nadine: Lower cupboards, drawers, silverware.

Marion: Clean ice-box, store-room, grocery bin, sink. Send out laundry.

SAT & SUN MEALS

Nadine
Phil
Alex
Marion
Lucile

Signed: MAW!

Philomene Bourassa Hood, Watkins Hall 1935–39, *University of Kansas Scrapbook,* 1935–1971, p. 42, Elizabeth Miller Watkins Legacy Collection #843, Kansas Historical Society, online at kansasmemory.org/item/223487/page/71.

T.M. James and Sons China Company of Kansas City, Missouri, shipped the order on June 24, 1926, "plates, cups, etc., marked 'Syracuse.'" The silver ordered was to be engraved "Watkins Hall."

— Spencer Research Library, Elizabeth Watkins Papers, RH MS 1, Box 166, 1926

Article 3 — KITCHENETTES

Section I: Kitchenettes must be in order before leaving them after each meal or at any special time (such as candy making, etc.).

Section II: Kitchenettes must be closed at 10:30 o'clock every night except Friday and Saturday. On Friday and Saturday nights they must be closed by 11 o'clock.

Section III: Kitchen shifts may be done Tuesday night before 10:30 o'clock and by special permission from the kitchen head on Friday night.

Section IV: Broken dishes must be reported to the kitchen head immediately and the kitchen head reports breakage at the first of the month, at which time broken dishes are to be paid for.

Article 4 — LAUNDRY ROOM

Section I: The laundry must be closed at 10:00 p.m. every night except Saturday. No laundering shall be done on Sunday except a pair of hose and pressing one dress before 10:00 a.m. Ironing may be done on Saturday until 11:00 p.m.

— **Hope Crittenden** and **Virginia Van Order,** *Inside Watkins,* University of Kansas, 1943, reprinted 2011, p. 15, Kitchen 8 Archives

Uses for the roof deck (balcony) on the second floor, the roof of the first-floor sun porch, have varied over the years. **Marion Horn, Dorothy Hendriksen,** *and* **Philomene Bourassa,** *roommates, look down from the roof deck to the sidewalk below;* **Dorothy Trekell** *and* **D.J. Willcutte** *pose with their tennis racquets; and* **Philomene Bourassa** *dries her hair in the sunshine, circa 1938.*

The study rooms could provide a place for quiet study, as for **Corrine Martin Ervin** *(left), Watkins Hall 1936–40, or a gathering place for fun (right).*

The walls of the second and third floors are finished in a mottled blue and gray with a blue border. Eight study rooms and a [sleeping] dormitory are on each of these floors. An infirmary is on the second . . . Each study room is furnished with a study table, rug, dresser, two lamps and three chairs.

— *University Daily Kansan*, September 14, 1926

Map by Miss Marjorie Whitney, KU faculty member for 40 years and chair of the Department of Design 1939–1968. This map is thought to have been drawn during her senior year at KU.

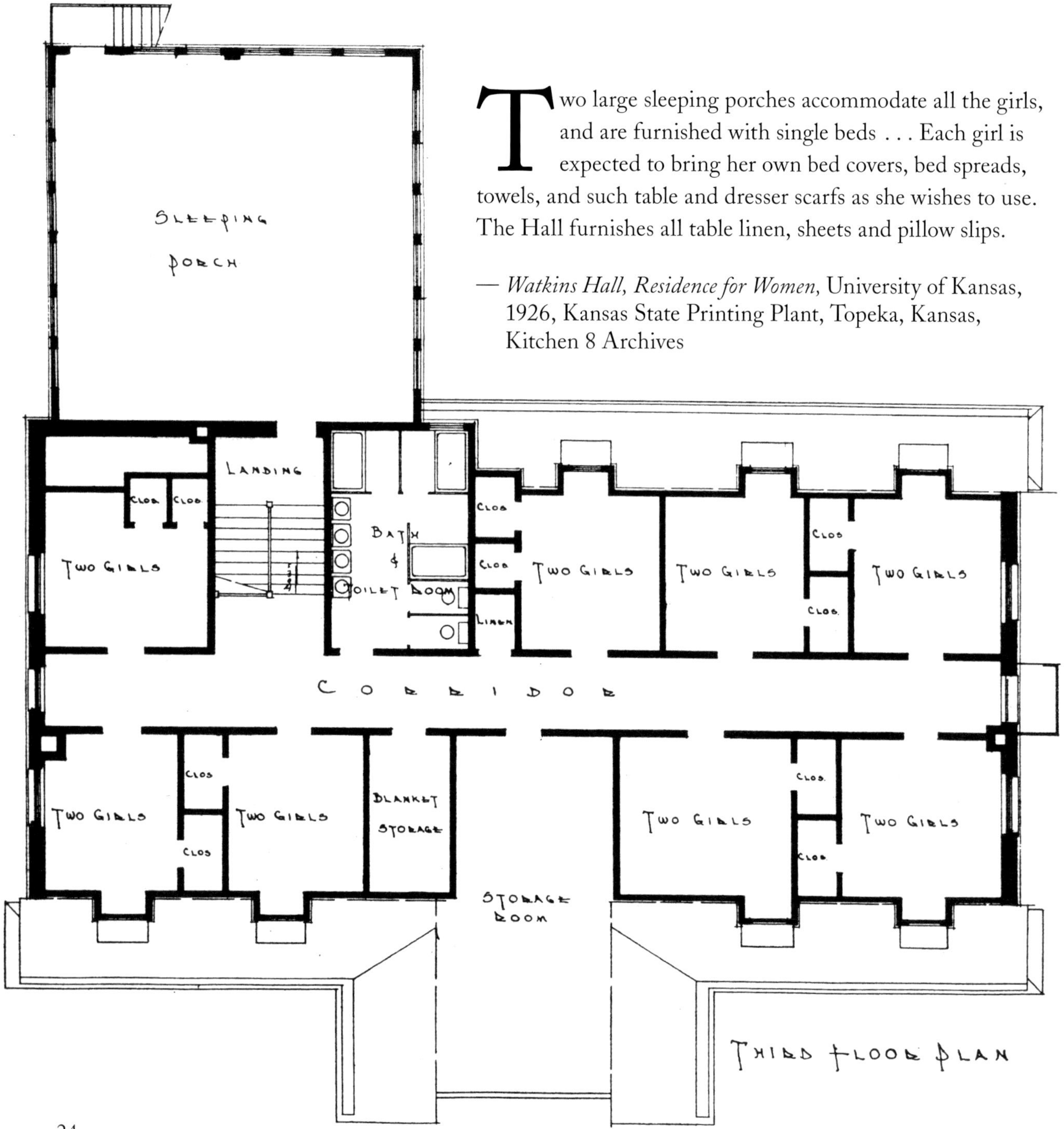

Two large sleeping porches accommodate all the girls, and are furnished with single beds . . . Each girl is expected to bring her own bed covers, bed spreads, towels, and such table and dresser scarfs as she wishes to use. The Hall furnishes all table linen, sheets and pillow slips.

— *Watkins Hall, Residence for Women,* University of Kansas, 1926, Kansas State Printing Plant, Topeka, Kansas, Kitchen 8 Archives

One girl, known as the "proctor" sees that the rest get up when the alarm rings — her job is probably one of the most difficult in the house.

— *The Graduate Magazine,* University of Kansas, April 1937, p. 15

Article 6 — RISING HOURS

Section I: Rising hours on Monday, Tuesday, Wednesday, Thursday, Friday, and Saturday shall be 7:00 o'clock; on Sunday it shall be 8:00 o'clock.

Section II: Floor proctors shall report to the executive board all persons still in bed ten minutes after the alarm has sounded.

— **Hope Crittenden** and **Virginia Van Order,** *Inside Watkins,* University of Kansas, 1943, reprinted 2011, p. 16, Kitchen 8 Archives

Perhaps [the funniest thing that ever happened] was the Sunday morning when **Alice Paden** decided to climb out of the sleeping porch to get on a painter's scaffolding— and found she could not climb back in? We took pictures before we had to give up and holler for help.

— **Philomene Bourassa Hood,** Watkins Hall 1935–39, Alumnae Tea Memory Card, Kitchen 8 Archives

Watkins Hall in winter, taken from atop Old Fraser Hall in 1935

In 1939, **Leora DeFord** said a lively [sleeping porch] hot-cold debate raged at Watkins as "there were the inevitable few who wanted some windows open in winter for fresh air." From this debate a new rule emerged: "You may only open the window by your bed." At Miller, **Nancy Arnold** always hoped not to have a bunk close to a "fresh air fiend or I'd freeze during the night." **Creta Carter Nichols,** on the other hand, liked sleeping with the window opened. "I loved hearing the flags on top of Fraser Hall flapping and popping in the wind as I fell asleep" and sleeping "under piles of my grandmother's quilts."

— *Kitchen 8 Newsletter,* March 2007, p. 17

Miller Hall, the latest gift to the University of Mrs. Elizabeth Watkins, is rapidly taking form beside its 10-year-old sister, Watkins Hall . . .

The sister houses, alike in almost every detail, are probably the only ones exactly of their kind in the nation . . . Residence in Watkins Hall, since its opening ten years ago, has been awarded by the University Scholarship Committee on the basis of scholarship, financial need, and character. Each year the number of applicants for the 39 vacancies in the Hall has increased tremendously. Applications begin pouring in to the committee long before the scholarships are formally announced.

Now with the opening of the new Miller Hall, 40 more scholarships will be available. . . .

Room rent at $13.50 a semester and board which averages from $5 to $10 a month are perhaps reasons enough for the increasing number of applications for Watkins Hall each year. The room rent is paid to the University, but the girls do their own cooking and thus manage their own food bills. Perhaps the most unique feature of the whole hall is the system of kitchens. There are seven of them and there will likewise be seven in the new house. . . .

The work of keeping the four floors of the Hall immaculate falls entirely to the 39 girls. The routine of the Hall works so smoothly that the house is cleaned completely by eight o'clock every morning. The girls get up at 6:30 and each one has a specified "shift" which is her part in keeping the house clean. . . .

A housemother, selected and paid by Mrs. Watkins, directs the house and acts as chaperon. . . . The University furnishes the house with heat, water, and electricity, and pays for the laundering of the house linen.

Many of the students in Watkins Hall have been able to remain in school only because of their scholarships there . . . they manage to maintain high scholastic averages. This year alone, four seniors in the Hall were elected to membership in Phi Beta Kappa.

— *The Graduate Magazine,* April 1937, pp. 14–15

In the thirties, public funds, like the weather, dried up. Buildings [at KU] came now from a single benefactor, Mrs. Elizabeth Watkins . . . Enrollment dropped and funding was slashed. Most students now combined study with whatever job they could find . . . Mrs. Watkins' gift of a second women's cooperative hall was timely in 1937.

— Virginia Adams, et al., *On the Hill, A Photographic History of the University of Kansas*, 3rd. ed. (Lawrence, KS, University Press of Kansas, 2007), p. 93

This portrait of Frank Miller is in the living room of Miller Scholarship Hall.

The new dormitory, designed as a duplicate of Watkins Hall which houses 39 women, will be completed and ready for use by September, 1937. Miller hall [is] named in memory of Frank Miller, a brother to Mrs. J. B. Watkins, and a University benefactor. Mr. Miller established a fund of $50,000, the income of which is donated to needy male students of the University of Kansas.

— *Building Scrapbook,* University Archives, Spencer Research Library, 56/14, 1937

As Miller hall nears completion, the "skyline" of east campus is attaining a new appearance. The hall is to be finished early in June and ready for women at the beginning of the next school year. It will be similar to Watkins hall, except that the internal structure is steel.

— *Building Scrapbook,* University Archives, Spencer Research Library, 56/14, 1937

Although the same blueprints were used for both halls, the "hospital room" built on the second floor of Watkins was changed to a study room for "two girls" in Miller. With Mrs. Watkins' gift of a student hospital to KU in 1931, built just west of the Outlook and Watkins Hall, she must have felt the health needs of the students were met. This allowed Miller to be publicized as a hall for 39 women, rather than 37 for Watkins.

Eleanor Roosevelt, on October 24, 1938, wrote in her nationally syndicated newspaper column "My Day,"

"We stopped for a few minutes at a girl's dormitory run on a cooperative plan where $15 a month covers all living expenses and, at the same time, the girls receive excellent training in housekeeping. To remain in the house they must have better than a 'B' average in their school work. This means that the leaders of the future are probably going through on this basis."

First Lady Eleanor Roosevelt leaves Miller Hall, flanked by a Kansas Highway Patrol security officer and Miller Hall president ***Sophia Schellenberg****.*

"I do not find fitting words to express my affectionate interest in these young people, but my hope is that, while enjoying life to the full, they will not fail to take advantage of every opportunity for effective preparation for the serious tasks which life must certainly bring to them. I shall leave them my most cordial good wishes."

— **Elizabeth Miller Watkins,** letter to Olin Templin, Kansas University Endowment Association Secretary, *Kansas City Times,* June 5, 1939

Elizabeth Josephine Miller Watkins
January 21, 1861–June 1, 1939

In the death of Mrs. J.B. Watkins, the University and Lawrence lose their greatest benefactress.

Mrs. Watkins' benefactions represented well-matured plans which had grown in her mind thruout the years. She not only had great sympathy and imagination, but great practical business judgment. Her counsel is said to have contributed greatly to the business success of her husband, Mr. Watkins.

The University mourns not only a great benefactress, but a beloved friend.

— Chancellor E.H. Lindley, *Lawrence Journal World,* June 1, 1939, p. 1

PALL-BEARERS
HONORARY
CHANCELLOR E. H. LINDLEY
DR. M. T. SUDLER
OLIN TEMPLIN
HUGH MEANS A. D. WEAVER
T. C. GREEN W. C. SIMONS
I. J. MEAD
ACTIVE
DR. R. I. CANUTESON
E. H. TAYLOR DICK WILLIAMS
A. B. WEAVER DOLPH SIMONS
T. J. SWEENEY, JR.
RAYMOND F. RICE
A. B. MITCHELL
C. B. RUSSELL
GENE HARRIS

Crossing The Bar

Sunset and evening star,
And one clear call for me!
And may there be
no moaning of the Bar
When I put out to sea.
\+ + + + + +
For tho' from out our bourne
of Time and Place
The flood may bear me far.
I hope to see my Pilot—
face to face,
When I have crost the bar.
—Tennyson

SERVICES
FOR
ELIZABETH M. WATKINS
BORN
JANUARY 21, 1861
NEW PARIS, OHIO
PASSED AWAY
JUNE 1, 1939
LAWRENCE, KANSAS
SERVICES HELD
AT
FIRST PRESBYTERIAN CHURCH
JUNE 3, 1939
CLERGYMEN
REV. THEO. H. ASZMAN
CHANCELLOR E. H. LINDLEY
INTERMENT
PRIVATE

IN MEMORIAM

Mrs. Elizabeth Watkins believed in us. She based her philosophy of life on a sincere faith in the college youth of this University. . . .

Well-beloved by students and fellow citizens, Mrs. Watkins was a modest benefactress who was known by her actions and unselfish open-handedness. . . .

Following the American dream, Mrs. Watkins chose education as the best answer to the problems of a democracy, and used her wealth to further its interests. She ever sought to transform desires into actualities in planning for a greater University. . . .

Despite our doubts and fears concerning our future, there is an undeniable inspiration in knowing that members of preceding generations are trusting in us. We must justify that trust.

—*University Daily Kansan,* June 4, 1939, p. 2

Mrs. Stayton was the first housemother employed by Elizabeth Watkins to chaperon Miller Hall. She was at the bedside when Mrs. Watkins passed away June 1, 1939.

— *University Daily Kansan,* June 1, 1939

[During her life, Mrs. Watkins personally decided the rent her residents were to pay. She further provided, on her death:]

That the rental or fees charged occupants of said dormitory shall at all times be in such reasonable amounts as shall be within the ability of self-supporting students to pay, and shall not exceed the sum of Three Dollars ($3.00) per month without . . . the unanimous written consent of a committee composed of C.E. Friend, A.B. Weaver and Dick Williams, or their successors, such successors to be named by the surviving members of said committee.

— Deed on Record No. 118, conveying Watkins Hall to the Kansas Board of Regents, November 1926

Elizabeth was an astute business woman. When she inherited J.B.'s estate, in 1921, it was valued at $2.4 million. She proceeded to:

- Build and furnish Watkins Hall
- Build and equip Watkins Hospital for students at KU
- Build and furnish Miller Hall
- Build and furnish a Nurses Home for the student hospital
- Build and equip Lawrence Memorial Hospital for the citizens of Lawrence

When Elizabeth passed away, in 1939, her estate was reported to be valued at $3 million.

— **Mary Burchill,** Elizabeth Miller Watkins' biographer

[Most important in her will, however, is the twelfth section, where Elizabeth designates $250,000 for a trust]

"to invest and reinvest the same . . . to use the income therefrom perpetually for the maintenance, upkeep and operation of Watkins Hall and of Miller Hall . . . the net income from said entire trust fund to be divided between said Watkins Hall and said Miller Hall, equally, share and share alike."

Elizabeth's will shows a generous heart to many. She gives Watkins Hall "the marine oil painting in my living room (Sunset at Long Beach, *by Richard Dey De Ribcowski)" which still hangs in Watkins Hall today and "to Miller Hall . . . the velvet tapestry* (Colonial Picture of Musicians) *hanging over the mantel in my living room."*

Watkins housemother, Mrs. Esterly, greets students at the front door. Elizabeth Watkins personally selected and paid all housemothers for both halls until her death.

During my freshman year, 1941–42, my housemother was Mrs. Stayton. She had been a personal friend of Mrs. Watkins and was therefore very aware of Mrs. Watkins' wishes for the halls she gave to the University of Kansas and their scholarship residents. Mrs. Stayton often spoke of her friend and how Mrs. Watkins regretted not being able to afford a college education when she was young, and her great satisfaction in being able to make it possible for talented girls of limited means to attend through the use of their scholarship hall awards.

— **Ruth Green Saffel,** Miller Hall 1942–46, letter to Judge Jack Murphy, February 1, 2000, Kitchen 8 Archives

We had . . . a housemother, Mother Willard, who taught us proper manners. Being a farm girl I had never eaten chicken with a fork before. I learned.

— **Arlone Brown Child,** Watkins Hall 1954–57, *Thank You, Elizabeth Miller Watkins, 2001,* Kitchen 8 Archives

My favorite Watkins memory? Tea with Mother Willard, in her elegant small apartment. A glimpse she gave us of being a lady! Showing us how to listen, be practical and gracious. "You can do it all," she said.

— **Donna Holm Fisher,** Watkins Hall 1946–49, Alumnae Tea Memory Card, 2011, Kitchen 8 Archives

Having come to College presumes a rightness of personal conduct and particularly in a Hall whose requirements for admission are high. . . . The character and standing of this place is dear to us all and must be maintained and protected — A GOOD NAME IS RATHER TO BE CHOSEN THAN GREAT RICHES — is just as true now as it was in the time of Solomon or Caesar.

— **Mother Lena Hayden Esterly,** Watkins Hall housemother, *Thoughts on Behavior at Watkins,* Kitchen 8 Archives

[O]ur house mother was a delightful and very proper lady in the old-fashioned sense of the word, and she was concerned that Watkins Girls not appear "common." When she saw one of us smoking while walking through the living room or sun porch, she would look quite pained and say, "Gulls!" (I'm sure she meant "girls" but it came out "gulls") "If you must smoke, DON'T travel with your cigarette!"

— **Allie K. Grove Spaulding,** Watkins Hall 1949–52, Alumnae Tea Memory Card, 2011, Kitchen 8 Archives

Watkins housemother Lena Hayden Esterly with her dog, Poquita

Housemothers ate their lunch and evening meals with the young women residents, rotating through each of the seven kitchens. The cook, or hostess, prepared the meal, following closely the Watkins Book of Etiquette *from 1958, which states the housemother "is always seated first."*

Watkins Scholarship Hall, class of 1945–46

In the fall of 1945, when I arrived at Watkins Hall, I was impressed with the fact that it was a beautiful "home" instead of a dorm without personality. The welcoming front hall with a gracious stairway to the second floor, the lovely living room with piano, the warm and bright sun room, told me I would be happy in this home. Having grown up with three sisters, the thought of living with nearly fifty sisters in a home appealed to me. The college years are a time of maturing for "girls" just out of high school. It is a short time before career, marriage and family absorb most of their lives. It is a time to develop life long friendships and bonds with young women. My memories of a roomful of girls gathered for a celebration, a gabfest or serious discussions of life, careers, and marriage have stayed with me. The small kitchens for family size meals were a time for discussing the day's events and personal feelings. It is there, Living With Girls, that Elizabeth's Daughters mature into her vision of Strong Women with Caring Hearts.

— **Roselyn Skonberg George,** Watkins Hall 1945–48, personal communication, Kitchen 8 Archives

With forty women — all of us talkers — we must insist upon keeping to regulation that no telephone conversation shall continue longer than five minutes. This is only fair to everybody concerned. If there is a reason for a longer conference, please make an appointment with your friend and have a face-to-face interview.

— **Mother Lena Hayden Esterly,** Watkins Hall housemother, 1940, Kitchen 8 Archives

In 1939, upperclass women made that [answering phone] chore a little more challenging for the freshmen. According to **Leora DeFord,** they would make the freshman answer the phone "with a silly little jingle ending with 'Who in the *Hall* do you want?'"

— *Kitchen 8 Newsletter,* March 2007, p. 15

Being only children, our time at Watkins taught us about sharing and living with others. We learned to cook. We developed lifelong friendships. We had round-robin letters among our classmates until a few years ago (over 50 years!)

— **Helen Stormont Browne** (left), Watkins Hall 1942–45 and **Virginia Van Order Thomas** (right), Watkins Hall 1942–46, personal communication, Kitchen 8 Archives

There had been a great amount of talk about the war in Europe. When we in Watkins Hall were gathered to hear President Roosevelt announce our declaration of war in 1941, it took on a new, horrible reality. Some of the senior girls were engaged to be married and were in tears. And some of their young men were killed in battle. Patriotism was high, and it was called World War II, "A War to Make the World Safe for Democracy."

The Dean of Men called an all-student convocation at the University. He spoke of how much we were all going to be needed in the work force in this country, and urged us to be serious students and graduate as early as possible. I had decided to major in Bacteriology and wanted to be a medical laboratory technician in a hospital. The courses were difficult but interesting and rewarding.

— **Mary Eileen Griffiths Bennett,** Watkins Hall 1940–44, *My Story,* Florence, Italy, 2006

A journalism major at KU, **Doris Kent Fox** (Watkins Hall 1935–37) . . . became an advertising manager for the Marshall Field stores in Chicago. At 22, she went on a "grand tour" of Europe and stayed to cover the fashion openings in Paris for the United Press. The day that she sailed for home on the Athenia, Hitler's army invaded Danzig. Two days later Britain declared war on Germany and that evening, at twilight, the Athenia was torpedoed. Doris was rescued and taken to Ireland.

— *Watkins 60th Anniversary Book,* October 1986, Kitchen 8 Archives

[Ruth Warren Wilkin, Watkins Hall 1938–40, remembers] "having tea with Mrs. Watkins in her home; the visit from First Lady Eleanor Roosevelt; . . . how upset I was when a fellow student went to Spain to fight Franco and was killed." [Before the U.S. entered WWII] "I remember how concerned we were about the possibility of the United States being involved in the war in Europe. I joined a Peace March on campus to protest that involvement."

— *Kitchen 8 Newsletter,* February 2008, pp. 17, 19

After **Helen Martin Gille**s [Miller Hall 1939–42] graduated from KU medical school, she did her residency in California, where her husband, 4F on account of an old football injury, was working on his doctorate in chemistry at the University of California-Berkley. Although she knew her husband was also working on a "secret government project," she didn't realize until the day the atomic bomb was dropped that he had been working on the Manhattan Project. "On the day the bomb was dropped, he went out and bought every newspaper he could find," she said. "That's when I figured out what he had been working on."

— *Kitchen 8 Newsletter,* 2008, p. 21

***June Montgomery,** Watkins Hall 1943–47, and her brother Jim in 1944*

Joyce Bourassa, Watkins Hall 1943–47, with her fiancé, Tony Wauro

I lived at Watkins 1946–49. . . . A truly remarkable living experience, one I think that uniquely prepared me for the diverse world I would live in. The colors, language, customs and cultures brought to the table, moving through the rooms . . . a whole education in itself, fleshing out the one I was receiving in the classroom.

— **Donna Holm Fisher,** Watkins Hall 1946–49, personal communication, Kitchen 8 Archives

"No matter how cold it was you couldn't wear pants or jeans to class." Roselyn recalled, adding that long skirts and coats became the winter fashion. Women could wear pants on campus during the weekends since there were no classes, however Roselyn learned the hard way that the growing post-WWII male student body did not like that look. "I wore jeans and a long shirt once and the Vets started hollering as I walked across campus," Roselyn said. "I snuck back to Watkins on the underside by Potter's Lake."

— **Roselyn Skonberg George,** Watkins Hall 1945–48, *Kitchen 8 Newsletter,* April 2014, p. 10

Maurine Waterstradt Adams, Watkins Hall 1941–45, remembers "From Dec. 15th (Pearl Harbor) my freshman year until after graduation, we were at war. We did not have a normal college experience. We shared the campus with the machinist mates, the V-12 and other military units. Perhaps sharing in pinning and engagement announcements qualified as a tradition. Those were happy times."

— Alumnae Tea Memory Card, 2010, Kitchen 8 Archives

Marilyn Whiting Thomas, Watkins Hall 1943–47, recalls after the war, there were so many returning soldiers to campus that living space became very crowded. She believes that is when the Watkins Hall "hospital room" on the second floor and the "guest room" on the first floor became study rooms for women. KU's student population went from 4,000 in 1939 to 12,000 just 7 years later, in 1946.

— 2013 Kitchen 8 Annual Meeting comments, Kitchen 8 Archives

"The housemother taught us etiquette, the officers taught us cleaning," remembered **Gayle Barry Matchett,** a "Watkins girl" from 1955–57. "But the memories were made in the small kitchens of Watkins Hall, learning to cook together. This cemented our friendships far more than any social life."

— John H. McCool, "The Girls Who Must Travel Up-hill," 2004, www.kuhistory.com

For Miller Hall Mrs. Watkins ordered R. Wallace silver "stamped in script 'MH'" from Jules Grogan of the Missouri China Company of Kansas City, Missouri. Note the china in the cabinet. Each spring, Watkins and Miller Halls hold an alumnae tea and these teacups are still in use at Miller Hall.

Jo Easter Longhofer, Miller Hall 1944-48, remembers making a double batch of donuts near closing hours one Sunday evening and having to enlist the help of a number of girls in order to sneak the donuts up the fire escape to avoid passing Mother Roche, who stood by her door and watched as girls went up to their rooms at closing hours. (No food was allowed upstairs!)

— *75 Years of Miller, 75 Years of Recipes,* **Staci Ashcraft,** 2012

Joyce Klemp Browder, Watkins Hall 1954–58, recalls her favorite Watkins tradition was "singing grace before meals."

— Alumnae Tea Memory Card, 2010, Kitchen 8 Archives

Sunday dinner will be a dress occasion — heels and hose. It will be understood that no jeans or shorts will be worn at the evening meals without reason, except on Saturday.

— *Meet Miller,* Revised 1955, Kitchen 8 Archives

Jeans, bermudas, shorts or slacks are **never** worn in the living room! The one exception to this rule is housemeeting.

— *The Watkins Book of Etiquette,* 1958–59 Etiquette Committee, **Carol Plumb,** chair, Kitchen 8 Archives

Housemother Julia Willard at dinner honoring senior girls, Council Room of Watkins Hall, 1958

Telephone shift consisted of answering the telephone and front door, using the buzzer system to alert residents of an incoming phone call or arrival of a guest. It was done from a small desk on the first floor of each hall. By the 1960s, two phone lines had been installed for the forty-nine women in each hall.

Jo Wiens Harbert (Watkins Hall 1955–59) recalls that 49 women had to share 2 phones, a point that left Watkins' Resident Assistant "blown away" when Jo visited Watkins a couple of years ago. "I pointed to the walls at the top of the stairs where the communication holes were back in the 1940s and 50s," she said. "Old timers like me could remember how the girl on duty would ring the bell code to call someone to the hole in the wall and tell her if she had a call." Jo noticed during her visit that all of the communication holes had been covered over, except for the one in the basement and the RA had no idea what it had been for. . . . Today every study room has a phone and most Watkins/Miller women also have cell phones . . . which sometimes makes phone duty a lonely endeavor.

— *Kitchen 8 Newsletter,* March 2007, p. 14

You will have a 'phone shift for one hour a day for one half-semester (nine weeks) during the year, and one evening 'phone shift about once every two months.

— *Meet Miller,* Revised 1955, p. 5, Kitchen 8 Archives

We always remember Mother Roche's admonition: "Now girls, a gentle squeeze on the arm is sufficient."

— **Mary Gosney-Lancaster,** Miller Hall 1957–58, *Kitchen 8 Newsletter*, February 2008, p. 13

For the most part, we Watkins women believed we were in charge of our own lives and that our futures depended on us . . . [W]e were in college because we had decided to take charge of our own lives and to propel ourselves into a future of opportunity and challenge . . . We believed that our lives, for the most part, depended on what we did with our innate gifts. But I will never forget that, in addition to our belief in ourselves, at Watkins we thrived in the atmosphere of support, appreciation, respect and encouragement we gave each other.

— **Creta Carter Nichols,** Watkins Hall 1955–57, *Kitchen 8 Newsletter,* March, 2007, p. 12

Miller Hall was the first scholarship hall to be integrated. We took a vote as to whether we wished to integrate. Our hall must have won, as we received two black students in 1955 . . . [They] were accepted fully into life there . . . I do remember a few of us and **Harriett [Lattimore,** Miller Hall 1955–59] went downtown to eat one evening and the waitress refused to serve us.

— **Pat Gardner Stein,** Miller Hall 1953–57, personal communication, Kitchen 8 Archives

Labeled "K-6," these women are all members of kitchen number 6 in Watkins Hall in 1949, again showing how these kitchen groups become like a small family. Left to right are: ***Virgina Blauvelt, Emily Clark, Shirley Ann Thomson, Mary Lou Auchard, Patti Lappin, Norma Hawkins,*** *and* ***Donna Hobein.***

Birthe Madsen Liisberg, Watkins Hall 1958–59, counts in her Watkins memories . . . "a line of happy faces welcoming me in the middle of the night when I arrived all the way from Denmark."

— *Watkins 60th Anniversary*, October 10–12, 1986, Kitchen 8 Archives

Move-in Day, 1969, at Watkins Hall. Many freshmen had never seen Watkins or Miller before this day and were delighted at their beautiful new "home."

Sue Hubert, Watkins Hall 1964–68, writes "After 42 years, I'm not sure which traditions are still alive. 'Just passing through' the living room on the way to the sunporch while wearing slacks, shorts, jeans, bare feet or curlers, for instance, is a fond, though thankfully passe', memory from my days there. We weren't supposed to be there unless properly dressed—meaning skirt or dress and no curlers. We were sometimes 'just passing through' for an hour or more."

— Alumnae Tea Memory Card, 2010, Kitchen 8 Archives

Dorothy Sloan Holmes, Watkins Hall 1964–67, remembers as her favorite Watkins tradition "leaving "MCWCB" messages for my friends!" ("Man Called: Will Call Back")

— Alumnae Tea Memory Card, 2010, Kitchen 8 Archives

Marie Mleynek Cling, Watkins Hall 1962–64, remembers "As for sledding down the Lawrence Hills, we just took large cookie sheets out of our 'stock up' kitchen and used them as sleds right behind Watkins Hall."

— Alumnae Tea Memory Card, 2011, Kitchen 8 Archives

Those were interesting times — lots of changes. We did away with the demerit system, had vegetarian and no-cook kitchens, had men in the rooms, fed sandwiches to the firemen who tried to put out the student union fire, watched rifle-carrying national guardsmen enforce the 10 p.m. curfew, watched various campus marches that were anti-war and pro-civil rights. It was, after all, the 60s!

— **Ola Stover Faucher,** Watkins Hall 1967–71, *Kitchen 8 Newsletter,* February 2008, p. 17

The KU Campanile, with the Kansas Union burning to the east, April 20, 1970

I came to Watkins in the fall of 1969, full of excitement and questions. . . . Fall progressed and the Vietnam War protests progressed in Lawrence. From peaceful, solely student gatherings the momentum increased until they were unrecognizable events that were nation-wide news, culminating in violence and the burning of our Student Union. We Watkins Women tended the firefighters with sandwiches and coffee and wondered at the view from our window. The next day, a new view was added to the window: a very young National Guard soldier. He looked to be about our age, fully armed and incredibly, he was guarding us. It was hard to tell who was more frightened.

— **Norma Decker Hoagland,** Watkins Hall 1969–71, *Kitchen 8 Newsletter*, May 2006, p. 13

Students assisted the firemen at the Kansas Union fire.

My Aunt Helen [**Dr. Helen Martin Gilles,** Miller Hall 1939–42], who lived in Miller when the Japanese attacked Pearl Harbor and the United States entered WWII, said her "most vivid memories" of the hall included "animated" discussions on the hot topics of the day. The same was true at Watkins in the 1970s, as the Vietnam War continued. In fact, I remember sit-ins on the lawn in front of Strong Hall to protest the war. And lest I forget, I also lived at Watkins during the Watergate era. I imagine, during this election year and while the war in Iraq continues, that "animated" discussions of current events continue today at Watkins and Miller.

— **Elizabeth Ervin Boman,** Watkins Hall 1971–75, *Kitchen 8 Newsletter*, February 2008, p. 2

The early 70's seemed to be marked by a little more questioning of authority and a little less automatic acceptance of "because-we've-always-done-it-this-way," not only in the Hall but in society in general. One constant remained—the sense of community and camaraderie developed as we all learned to live together. Not for nothing did Chancellor Chalmers describe his scholarship hall neighbors to the north as "Commune Corners."

Watkins was a safe place for us to explore blending head and heart, practicing pragmatic and caring idealism. Coming at the end of the Viet Nam war and at a time when Virginia Slims commercials proclaimed audaciously "You've come a long way baby," the changes in American society during the 1970's filtered into Watkins Women's experiences. We may have come a long way, yet more of us needed not only the Hall award, we needed a first, sometimes second, job to follow our dreams. We experimented with different diets in the kitchens as well as schedules, and varied the time we spent together in our quasi-family kitchen group. Hall life did indeed mirror larger society in that sense. . . .

My first year, we had a married Resident Assistant in the housemother's apartment. It was "Doug and Roselyn" we invited to dinner once a week. . . . we learned to support each other in following our hearts whether or not they were planned or inadvertent "pioneering efforts." We learned how to be a cheering section. 1972 was the year the KU Marching Jayhawks first allowed women in the Marching Band. The next year a Watkins Woman played her baritone horn in the Marching Band—and we rejoiced. One year Carole [Smith] Carey made the Jayhawk yell leader squad—and we cheered also.

Though we weren't conscious of actively doing so, I think we worked towards a more encompassing and pragmatic feminism that fostered the total human, not just one aspect of a traditional, gender-based social behavior. . . .

Not only did we have education majors, English and German language majors, nursing and medical technology, we had pharmacy, occupational therapy, radiation biophysics and journalism. . . .

We rather proudly proclaimed a Miss Kansas for Watkins, as well as a couple of others who felt encouraged by her example to enter the contest for themselves. . . .

We laughed, and learned to laugh at ourselves. We learned to challenge institutions, and cross traditional lines even when it didn't always turn out the way we hoped it would. We helped support other Scholarship Hall's visions, and for the most part enjoyed doing it . . . .

These were *Watkins Women*? Yes, these were the early 1970's group. We'd gladly forego the bra-burning, just get us enough money in our paychecks to pay for the bras, the food on the table, the roof over our head, and tuition and books.

— **Susan Tara Masih,** Watkins Hall 1972–75, personal communication, Kitchen 8 Archives

Miller Hall, class of 1978

Lorra Tow *opens her birthday present at a surprise party in one of the kitchens of Miller Hall, 1974.*

One evening the women in Kitchen 3 were all sitting around the un-set table at 5:30 when the last person came in and sat in the last empty chair and wanted to know what was for supper. We told her we did not know and wanted to know what she had made. The cook for the evening forgot she was to cook! That evening we were all on the diet plate and had to fend for ourselves.

— **Barbara Jiricek Kennedy,** Watkins Hall 1974–78, Alumnae Tea Memory Card, 2011, Kitchen 8 Archives

"Sitting down every night to a home cooked meal and only having to cook and clean up 1 night a week" was the favorite kitchen memory of **Susan Harshaw Kissinger,** Watkins Hall 1970–74.

— Alumnae Tea Memory Card, 2011, Kitchen 8 Archives

More than a dozen 1970s alumnae held a reunion. . . . Every one attending the reunion also took a turn repeating her "buzz," the series of "dits" and "dahs" that let you know you had a call or gentleman waiting to see you downstairs. "Note that NO ONE had forgotten her buzz," **Pat Jolly Putnam** said.

— *Kitchen 8 Newsletter,* March 2012, pp. 16-17

Our beautiful, blonde student from Finland, **Toola Tusavingan,** loved my dinners. One time, she pushed away from the table, patting her slim stomach and declared, "Carole, if I was a man, I would marry you for your cooking!" Everyone laughed. I quipped, "When's the candle passing?" Best compliment I ever had!

— **Carole Smith Carey,** Watkins Hall 1970-74, Alumnae Tea Memory Card, 2011, Kitchen 8 Archives

Laura Shoffner Klover, Watkins Hall 1978–81, wrote her favorite tradition was "The use of Morse code to let a woman know she had a guest or phone call. Mine was dash-dot-dash. This tradition has probably long been replaced. There was one phone on each floor and that was it (besides the front desk phone.) Women took turns at phone duty. It worked pretty well."

— Alumnae Tea Memory Card, 2010, Kitchen 8 Archives

There was a diversity of background in these 50 women, some of us from farms, some from cities but all with a financial need and a desire for education. . . . Elizabeth Miller Watkins created an environment that brought out the best in us. She was a genius in the way she constructed the halls. The living spaces allowed for conversation and study. We questioned, we supported each other, we had drama and always, we cooked.

— **Cathie Fuller Miller,** Watkins Hall 1970–74, personal communication, Kitchen 8 Archives

Getting to know the international students broadened my world. This happened not only while I was in Watkins, by being in a kitchen and eating the interesting food **Johanna Bogadottir** prepared for us, but also as an adult, by giving me the opportunity to visit her in Iceland where I was introduced to her country on a very personal level, not just as a tourist on a tour.

— **Elizabeth Ervin Boman,** Watkins Hall 1971–75, personal communication, Kitchen 8 Archives

The Legend of the Llama: In the early 1970s a South American international student lived in Watkins. She could not afford a plane ticket home one Christmas break, though she desperately wanted to see her family. The women took up a collection to buy her a ticket. To show her gratitude, she brought back a pair of stuffed llamas. Since then, the llama has been the Watkins' mascot, and a symbol of what WWW [Wild Watkins Women] will do for each other.

— *Watkins Scholarship Hall Alumnae Newsletter,* Spring 2007, p. 6

Watkins Hall celebrated with two residents, ***Maria Elena Rodriguez*** *(pictured) and* ***Elena Wahbeh,*** *who became naturalized citizens of the United States during the 1970–71 academic year.*

Shauna Moore**, Watkins Hall 1981–85, wrote "When I think of Watkins, I think of a home away from home, lasting friendships, stairway chats, waiting to hear my buzz (sometimes to no avail!,) and late-night runs to Joe's [donuts]. Mostly, I think of a special place I miss, and think of often."

— *Watkins 60th Anniversary Book*, October 1986, Kitchen 8 Archives

Following the turbulent 1960s and changing times of the 1970s, a less-formal attitude was the "new norm" during the 1980s for both Watkins and Miller Halls.

***Venetta Abbott**, fifty-two-year-old freshman at Miller Hall and the "oldest student to have lived in the scholarship hall system," was featured in* Kansas Alumni, *June 1982. "I feel like more of an older sister," she said in reference to living with younger women in Miller. She was a court reporter and is pursuing a BGS in law-related fields at KU, the article reported.*

During the 1990s, **Alica [Thomas, Miller Hall 1990–94]** said that Millerites rediscovered a number of old traditions, including going to Joe's Place, which is the hall's annual dance. . . . But social events were not Alica's only memories of life at Miller; world events and social issues also had an impact. Alica said that the first Gulf War was an important memory. Also, while she lived at Miller two residents and their mothers disappeared, and it was later learned that they had joined a religious cult. According to Alica, the press attention to the story went on for weeks.

— *Kitchen 8 Newsletter,* February 2008, p. 5

Sharing a study room requires compromise and diplomacy, good life skills! Although the halls were designed originally for fewer women, two, three, and even four women to a study room now enables each hall to accommodate forty-nine women.

By the 1990s, the stairway evolved into a place for conversation and sharing, rather than its earlier use on formal occasions only.

Hawk Week progresses smoothly and I am finally adapting to the communal sleeping system. My sleepy senses now only acknowledge the annoying blare of my alarm clock; no longer do I jolt upright at the piercing rings of the other three billion alarms, for in my experience, the number of alarm clocks that go off each morning is directly proportional to the magnitude of my tiredness.

— **Gloria Cheng,** Watkins Hall 1990–93, *Watkins Scholarship Hall Newsletter,* Fall 1992, p. 7, Kitchen 8 Archives

Surely, no changes at Watkins/Miller have been more revolutionary than curfew and "gentlemen caller" rules. Back in the 1930s, **Philomene Bourassa Hood** says there were "university-wide women's closing hours" and Watkins residents had to produce a "signed parental permission slip in order to travel away from Lawrence or be absent from the hall overnight.". . .

[I]n the 1950s **Creta Carter Nichols** said men were only allowed in the lounge areas and kitchens. . . . She noted wryly, "I do not believe that the men had curfews, but this was the 1950s.". . . **Nadine Blair Kay** [Watkins Hall, 1956–60] remembers giving "Man on the Floor!!" warnings in her 2010 Alumnae Tea memory card, if a man were given permission by the house mother to go upstairs.

By the 1970s, **Janet Smith Calkins** [Watkins Hall, 1970–74] said Watkins was a time of "real change" as far as "gentlemen callers" were concerned. In addition to public areas, women were allowed to have male guests in their study rooms. . . . Although Watkins closed and locked the doors at night, through the magic of electronic keycards, women were free to come and go as they pleased 24 hours a day — no permission slips required.

Today, Watkins [and Miller] continue to have 24-hour open visitation, but the electronic keycards have been replaced by an electronic touchpad system. In addition, for security reasons, doors are now locked at all times.

— *Kitchen 8 Newsletter,* 2007, pp. 16–17

Along with changes in curfew and guests in the rooms, other changes were happening in the halls. Rent or fees for Watkins and Miller Halls was $27 in 1926. Forty-five years later, in 1971, rent was $95. Another forty-five years later, in 2016, it had reached $2,656.

— Original Deed to Watkins, 1926; *Watkins Hall Alumnae & Friends Newsletter,* August 1997; KU Department of Student Housing's History of Room and Meal Plan Rates

2011 Kitchen mates (left to right) ***Emily Katz, Kayla Eddins,*** *and* ***Sarah Greenup*** *have lunch in a defining feature of their hall: seven-woman kitchens, which Mrs. Watkins thought would encourage newly independent residents to learn to cook. Miller and Watkins both have seven kitchens; their alumnae group is "Kitchen 8."*

— Kansas Alumni, *March–April 2011, p. 22*

Living in Watkins Hall forever changed me. Even though I haven't lived there since 2009, I still feel like I could walk upstairs to my room or downstairs to my kitchen every time I walk through the door. I have to fight the urge to "tag in" and check my mailbox which is no longer mine, and I feel like I could run into some of my best friends right around the corner, even though they now live scattered across the states. Watkins just stays with you.

— **Laura Draxler Sixta,** Watkins Hall 2005–09, personal communication, Kitchen 8 Archives

Tisa Martinson, Watkins Hall 2007–09, writes, "There are a lot [of kitchen memories] to choose from, but certainly the most unusual one took place on April Fools Day. We all came down for breakfast only to discover all of the dishes were gone. And the silverware, too. It became quite the scavenger hunt. The silverware was stashed in the mailboxes, as well as in various containers, while the dishes were hidden in the scary GK [general kitchen] and unused cupboards, as well as lots of other places. Everyone thought it was a bit much, especially when the unknown perpetrators failed to put things back. In fact, we were still finding hidden stashes the next year! Since I didn't have anywhere to go that morning, though, I thought it was great entertainment."

— Alumnae Tea Memory Card, 2011, Kitchen 8 Archives

I fondly recall "The Candlelightings." When one of the girls got engaged, the hall would congregate in the living room, form a circle and turn out the lights. A candle was lit and we'd sing "The Sweetheart of Lilac Lane" as the candle was passed around the circle. It had to complete a whole rotation. Then the bride-to-be blew it out when next she received the candle. Sometimes it was expected but there were some real surprises, too.

— **Carole Smith Carey,** Watkins Hall 1970–74, Alumnae Tea Memory Card 2013, Kitchen 8 Archives

By 2009 candlelightings were no longer solemn ceremonies held only in the formal living room. ***Megan Krogh*** *and* ***Dory Cochran*** *celebrate with* ***Laura Draxler*** *(left to right) on the roof of the sun porch.*

—Watkins Hall Scrapbook, *2009*

The mystique of this beloved tradition may have become an inadvertent victim of the digital age of iPhones, Facebook and Twitter. Let me explain. At Miller, the first candlelighting of the year, and ever for some new residents went a little more like this: Everyone gathered in the darkened Miller living room. A diamond ring was tied to the lighted candle. The candle was passed around the circle once so we could all admire the ring. On the second time around, Miller Alumnae Chair **Emilyjane Pyle** blew out the candle and we all cheered. Emilyjane was engaged to her high school sweetheart . . . We know, we know, so what's new? [Her] grandmother lived in Miller in the 1940s and surely would have participated in the candlelighting ceremonies just like her granddaughter was doing more than 60 years later. Back in the 1940s it would not have been hard for a Miller woman to keep her engagement secret until she blew out the candle the second time around the circle. . . . in the age of Facebook there are no more secrets. Still, who doesn't love a good candlelighting even if you know what's coming the second time around the circle.

— **Kristina Nielander,** Miller Hall president, 2012–13, *Kitchen 8 Newletter,* 2013, pp. 23–24

In 1960 the entertainment was *'Singing in the Rain'* with (left to right) ***Pat Glendening, Carol Keeler, Judy Johnson,*** and ***Virginia Ryan.***

Miller Hall's signature party "Joe's Place" was first held in 1944 and the theme was a speakeasy. The invitations to the first dance, which sported a very selective guest list, told guests to "knock three times and ask for Joe." This traditional event evolved into a costumed dance, as these "black cats" (Jerry Niebaum and **Judy Johnson**) from 1960 show. It is still being held annually!

— www.millerhall.org

Joe's Place 1953 featured a can-can chorus line of ***Norma Davidson, Carol Kasper, Jo Rogers, Mary Schroeder, Nancy Meyers, Mary Fran Poe, Carol Hemphill, Marilyn Fuller,*** *and* ***Helen Haize.***

Terena DaSilva, Watkins Hall 2002–06, recalls her favorite Watkins tradition was "Heaven & Hell. The fact that most of the campus knows about it is pretty cool. It shows how united the women of Watkins are since it is their hard work that makes it all happen. They enjoy the whole day when everyone gets together and contributes."

— Alumnae Tea Memory Card, 2010, Kitchen 8 Archives

Bev Runkle, *dressed as the devil, and her roommate* ***Joyce Klemp*** *entertain "Cisco" at the 1956 Heaven and Hell party.*

Donna Holm Fisher, Watkins Hall 1946–49, remembers "I was the Social Chairman the *very* first year for the Heaven and Hell Dance. Now *that* was a lot of fun."

— Alumnae Tea Memory Card, 2009, Kitchen 8 Archives

Freshmen ***Emily Hane, Stevi Ballard,*** *and* ***Lynne Lammers*** *dressed as Peter Pan, Wendy, and Tinkerbell for the 2007 Heaven and Hell party.*

Traditions Night in September was a lot of fun as we learned and celebrated the past with stories, memories, old hall songs, and a surprise visit from the spirit of Elizabeth Watkins in the form of Historian **Mary Emerson.** Dressed in her proper black skirt and starched, high-collar blouse, Mrs. Watkins told residents why she started Watkins Hall and how important it is for us to be strong women.

— **Megan Krogh** and **Kim Moore,** Watkins alumnae co-chairs, *Kitchen 8 Newsletter*, February 2008, p. 12

Left to right are ***Mary Emerson, Kristina Nielander, Keeleigh Smith, Katie Kutsko,*** *and* ***Erin Christianson*** *standing by a portrait of Elizabeth Watkins in the Outlook.*

[In 2013, Kitchen 8 arranged for a tour of the Outlook, now the chancellor's residence. The Outlook had been Elizabeth's home for many years and is a special place to her "daughters" as the halls are right next door! As the *Lawrence Journal World* reported] "So the current residents . . . know about the woman whose gifts still allow them to live for a lower cost than they could anywhere else in Lawrence. Though [Mrs.] Watkins does not come each morning to make sure they've done their chores before they go to class, as she did decades ago, they still know her."

— *Lawrence Journal World*, April 27, 2013, pp. 1A–2A

Both Watkins and Miller Halls hold an alumnae tea each spring, inviting all alumnae to return to the halls to renew their ties and be entertained with music, poetry, and prose readings. In 2012 the alumnae were treated to a campanile recital by a current Watkins Hall resident.

*Carrying on Mrs. Watkins' wishes, Watkins resident **Katie Ellsworth** and Watkins alumna **Gayle Barry Matchett** are using real china at the 2012 Alumnae Tea.*

*At the Miller Hall Alumnae Tea in 2012, **Judy Johnson Niebaum,** Miller Hall 1958–61, Kitchen 8 Miller Hall campus coordinator, presented to the Miller women a poster-sized reproduction of a Miller kitchen photo from the 1950s. Those present at the tea suddenly realized they were using the same teacups that were on the shelf in the photo!*

I believe our alumnae connection with these young women does emphasize the intention of ongoing support that Elizabeth Miller Watkins planned for deserving students. And as one who benefitted from her generosity in "my day" I am happy to help to pass on her spirit of caring!

—**Judy Johnson Niebaum,** Miller Hall 1958–61, personal communication, Kitchen 8 Archives

In 2006, Watkins Hall residents and alumnae marched down Jayhawk Boulevard to Strong Hall, showing their support and thanks to Elizabeth Watkins.

Instead of simply hosting the Watkins Alumnae Tea that spring, we held a weekend extravaganza, on April 22–23, 2006, to celebrate the hall's 80th birthday. The weekend's festivities included a strong showing of Watkins residents at Kitchen 8's annual meeting and a march down Jayhawk Boulevard, reminiscent of the parade held for the 60th birthday celebration. That weekend was also the start of a new tradition — a gathering of residents and alumnae to lay flowers on Elizabeth Miller Watkins' grave.

— **Ali Bannwarth Zayas,**
Watkins Hall 2002–06,
personal communication,
Kitchen 8 Archives

For me, my whole Watkins experience can be encapsulated in a word: Family. Conversations around the kitchen table; taking about what we did that day and silly inside jokes that made me feel so at home. And at the Alumnae Teas it was like a huge reunion where I got to see and meet the extended family. An extended family of women who help each other travel up hill. Seeing Mrs. Watkins's dream keep going through generations of Watkins Women into the future because of that familial bond has had a huge impact on me. Now I know that I don't have to be famous or some type of government figure to make a difference, I just have to help my fellow women whenever I can. I had the privilege of planning three Alumnae Teas and helping with all of the events surrounding Lizzie's 150th birthday. Helping make those events happen and bringing all these amazing women together is something I won't ever forget and will always treasure. I got to form relationships with women who lived in the hall 5, 10, 30, 50 and even 70 years before me. Not many people I know count women who graduated in 1939 among their "college friends" but I do. I love that I got to be a part of passing on Mrs. Watkins legacy to a whole new group of women and that I can come back as an alumnae now and tell my stories. . . . Our experiences in Watkins seem to be timeless. . . . It doesn't matter when you lived in the hall, that family is here for you and always will be.

— **Sarah Greenup,** Watkins Hall 2008–11, personal communication, Kitchen 8 Archives

Alumnae and hall residents gather in 2006 at the gravesites of Elizabeth and J.B. Watkins.

Elizabeth Miller Watkins is many things: woman, daughter, secretary, wife, philanthropist, and hero to thousands of girls she never knew. I am one of those girls. . . . we visited Elizabeth's grave to pay our respects and thanks to her. We each talked about how Elizabeth had touched our own lives. . . . I felt so moved; I looked around and I realized that I was not standing there with housemates and alumnae, but with my sisters.

— **Mary Emerson Gomez,** Watkins Hall 2004–08, *Kitchen 8 Newsletter*, February 2008, p. 6

As all Miller and Watkins residents know, each hall has 7 small kitchens. Although the use of the 7 kitchens has evolved over time, they still remain an integral part of life and camaraderie within the halls. Our organization serves as a link between the past and present women of Miller and Watkins as a metaphoric "Kitchen 8."

— *Kitchen 8 website* 2011, www.kitchen8.org

KITCHEN 8

We are a volunteer group of friends and beneficiaries of Elizabeth Miller Watkins, dedicated to assisting financially needy, academically talented undergraduate KU women and preserving the story of Elizabeth Miller Watkins and her legacy.

Members of Kitchen 8 are alumnae of Watkins and Miller Halls, both of which were built and donated by Elizabeth Miller Watkins, and were the first of their kind in the nation.

Kitchen 8 had its beginnings in the 1980s when residents of Watkins and Miller solicited help from alumnae to get the deteriorating Halls repaired. Through the years, Kitchen 8 has been instrumental in getting upkeep and maintenance issues addressed and, initially, in getting Watkins and Miller Hall's rents reduced. When the alumnae learned that the residential scholarships had been greatly diminished by annual rent increases, K8 also began offering financial scholarships.

It has also embarked on an archival project to collect and preserve documents related to Elizabeth Miller Watkins and her legacy.

— *Kitchen 8 Newsletter*, May 2005, p. 1

In 2011, a group of current residents and alumnae gathered before Elizabeth's portrait in Watkins Hall. They are (left to right) ***Kayla Eddins, Molly Willow, Qiao Yi Chen, Norma Decker Hoagland, Hilary Schloemer, Dana Diec, Bev Runkle Benso,*** *and* ***Sarah Greenup.***

Leslie Mettenburg Moore, Watkins Hall 2003–07, wrote, "We were all recipients of a great gift, from a woman we didn't know, from a time before we existed. And what did we think we would gain [by the court petition against the bank holding the Watkins and Miller Hall Trust]? Physically, we hoped to stop the deterioration of the Watkins and Miller Halls — no one considered the possibility that the state of the Halls might actually *improve*, which they did! But more than that, we wanted Mrs. Watkins to know that her gift wasn't taken for granted, that we appreciated what she had done for us, and that we cared about the future of the women, who, like us, would find themselves on Lilac Lane. We wanted to continue her legacy."

— *Committee for the Preservation of Watkins and Miller Scholarship Halls at KU Newsletter*, Volume 4, Issue 2, October 2004, Kitchen 8 Archives

Since Kitchen 8 established the Elizabeth Miller Watkins Memorial Scholarship fund in 1999, it has awarded $330,600 to 91 deserving KU women.

Joyce Klemp Browder, Watkins Hall 1954–58, chair of the Scholarship Selection Committee, said in 2010 "Kitchen 8 established the [Elizabeth Miller Watkins Memorial Scholarship] fund for women attending KU as an expression of their appreciation for receiving an outstanding education through Elizabeth Miller Watkins' generosity and their desire to extend the opportunity they were given to today's young women."

— *Kitchen 8 Newsletter*, March 2010, p. 8

> Elizabeth Miller Watkins . . . was generous but not frivolous. . . . She gave a home to aspiring female KU students. . . . I feel I am walking through the gate she opened in my academic career and following her footsteps by making sure other women around me understand her influence and their opportunities and success as a result.
>
> — **Cayla Witty,** EMW Memorial Scholarship recipient, 2005, Watkins Hall 2003–07, *Kitchen 8 Newsletter*, May 2005, p. 5

[**Alica Thomas,** Miller Hall 1990–94, chair of Kitchen 8's Elizabeth Miller Watkins Memorial Scholarship Advisory Board reflects that] "Elizabeth Miller Watkins Scholars are the cream of the crop. They have participated in endless hours of volunteer work, in addition to their scholastic achievement and their outside employment. They are the epitome of what Mrs. Watkins envisioned for the scholarship halls."

— *Kitchen 8 website* 2014, www.kitchen8.org

I am grateful to have the opportunity to carry on Lizzie's work by serving on the K8 scholarship selection committee. The work is a joy because the applicants are wise and funny and in spite of overwhelming challenges, they have achieved amazing things. They have traveled (even with limited means) and they are making the world a better place. The work is difficult because there are so many with need who are so qualified.

— **Susan Harshaw Kissinger,** Watkins Hall 1970–74, Scholarship Selection co-chair, 2013 to present, personal communication, Kitchen 8 Archives

Janice Gartrell, *Watkins Hall 1939–42, established a trust which was added to the Kitchen 8 Elizabeth Miller Watkins Memorial Scholarship Fund in 2009. Janice wished to help young women, just as Mrs. Watkins had done.*

Every other year, Kitchen 8 holds a Career Day for the women of Watkins and Miller, with sessions of general interest such as resumé writing, business dinner etiquette, and business attire. Also, there is a chance for the residents to speak to alumnae from different career paths.

Watkins alumna **Elena Wahbeh,** *of Kansas City, Missouri, tells Watkins and Miller women about careers in physical therapy.*

Miller alumna **Dr. Annette Smith,** *a pulmonologist from St. Joseph, Missouri, talks with residents about medical careers.*

As President of Watkins Hall, I helped organize the first New Women Dinner held at Watkins Hall in August 2005. For the first time, new residents were introduced to the legacy of Elizabeth Miller Watkins the very same week they moved into the halls. Immediately, I noticed a new "Watkins spirit" in these new residents. This contagious spirit infected the old women in the hall as well.

— **Ali Bannwarth Zayas,** Watkins Hall 2002–06, personal communication, Kitchen 8 Archives

The New Woman Dinner for both Miller and Watkins Halls is held each fall as members of Kitchen 8 first meet the incoming freshmen and transfer students. A booklet about Mrs. Watkins is presented to each new resident, so that they begin their stay in the halls aware of her visionary work and her unique and great gift to each of them.

Celebrating Elizabeth Watkins' January 21 birthday each year, alumnae give gifts to both halls. Watkins Hall campus coordinator ***Bev Runkle Benso*** *presents gifts in 2013 (upper).* ***Claire MacLachlan*** *(center) and* ***Taylor Moody*** *(lower) show obvious delight at the 2015 party. A treat served alongside birthday cake is Jordan almonds, one of Elizabeth's favorites.*

With Elizabeth Miller Watkins as a common benefactor, Kitchen 8 and the Watkins Museum of History work together to share stories of her commitment to Lawrence. Activities for current Watkins and Miller scholarship hall residents and for alumnae are often held at the Watkins Museum, housed in a building that Mrs. Watkins' will ensured would be used for public benefit. Kitchen 8 and the Watkins Museum also collaborate to present programs that increase awareness of Mrs. Watkins' philanthropic activities and celebrate her support of KU students and the community in general.

— Steven Nowak, executive director, Watkins Museum of History, personal communication, Kitchen 8 Archives

Watkins and Miller residents and Kitchen 8 members join together several times a year for events to celebrate Mrs. Watkins' legacy of generosity that binds them together. After the 2009 K8 annual meeting, they gathered for a tour of the Watkins Museum of History. ***Ali Bannwarth Zayas, Kristen Cowan, Sarah Greenup, Joyce Klemp Browder,*** *and* ***Megan Krogh*** *(upper to lower) head up the stairs at the museum to see Jabez' private apartment.*

The National Park Service added the University of Kansas East Historic District to the register this month [January 2014]. The district covers the period of 1912–1963 and contains [eight of the University of Kansas' scholarship halls, the chancellor's residence, and Danforth Chapel].

"I can't tell you how many alumni have shared with me their fond memories of living in a scholarship hall or of getting married in Danforth Chapel. These places are central to the lives of so many Jayhawks, and we're pleased to be able to preserve these buildings and landscapes so that current and future students can have similar experiences while at KU," Chancellor Bernadette Gray-Little said.

— www.housing.ku.edu

Dr. Jerry Niebaum, retired assistant provost for Information Services at KU, member of Historic Mount Oread Friends, and friend of Kitchen 8, led a large group of K8 members, KU alumni, and students on a walking tour of the new East Campus Historic District, which includes Miller and Watkins Halls, as well as the Outlook.

From two, now twelve

The long history of scholarship halls is built on generous private gifts, starting with two from Elizabeth Miller Watkins . . . the first two halls of their kind in the country. Watkins was instrumental in the design and operation of this new type of housing. The scholarship hall community has since grown to 12, six for men and six for women.

— *KU Giving,* Winter 2012

On the 150th anniversary of her birth, it seems appropriate to do more than merely celebrate. Anyone who ever comes to KU, to teach or study or work, has heard Elizabeth Miller Watkins' name, maybe knows a tiny sketch of biography, perhaps has heard that some old lady way back in the day invented the whole concept of "scholarship halls," where good students could live for reduced rates in exchange for a few hours each week cooking and cleaning. . . .

She is not a name, she is not a scholarship hall, she is not an estate. She was so much more than money, and yet she guarded it zealously, disbursed it generously, used it wisely, and made advantages for others because of it.

— Chris Lazzarino, *Kansas Alumni,* March–April, 2011, p. 24

Each fall the women of Miller and Watkins Halls gather to remember Elizabeth Miller Watkins, who made this opportunity available for them, by speaking of her life and reciting together Elizabeth's Creed by candlelight.

Acknowledgments

Ralph Waldo Emerson said all history is biography. I am pleased to bring you the fourth book in the series "Biography of a Building," a story of two buildings, Watkins and Miller Scholarship Halls at the University of Kansas. The open door on the cover of this book is symbolic: although the building was the framework for Elizabeth Watkins' visionary idea, what happened inside was just as important as the building. She designed her scholarship halls to be a safe, empowering place where young women could dream, talk, be respected, and grow in a cooperative, supportive environment. The story of these buildings is told by the women who lived in them.

This year [2016] we celebrate the ninetieth anniversary of Watkins Hall, Elizabeth's forward-thinking experiment. Next year we celebrate Miller Hall's eightieth anniversary. Not only are the buildings still viable, but they are also to be renovated in the summer of 2016, ensuring more young women will enjoy these beautiful homes for years to come. The harvest from Elizabeth's idea and her gift continues.

My first thanks goes to Elizabeth Miller Watkins. I am one of thousands of grateful women whose life was changed due to her foresight and assistance. I grew up on a small family farm in Kansas and could not have attended college had it not been for my Watkins and KU scholarships.

In my journey to research and compile this book, Mary Burchill, fellow Watkins enthusiast, author, and biographer, has been a constant source of help and inspiration. Carol Shankel and Barbara Watkins, the editors, will have my thanks forever, for taking on a project with someone who had more enthusiasm than experience. Shala Stevenson, the book designer, made the pages come alive with true interest in the story we were telling. Historic Mount Oread Friends are truly friends, for publishing *Watkins and Miller Halls* in their "Biography of a Building" series on KU landmarks.

The real anchors of this book, besides Elizabeth, are the women of Kitchen 8, the alumnae organization for these halls. They shared their stories, their photos, and memories, so that readers would know how Elizabeth's two scholarship halls did exactly what she had envisioned: they transformed young girls into a supportive family of strong women. Thank you to all my Watkins and Miller sisters for your unfailing support, especially Gayle Barry Matchett. Because of their actions in response to the condition of the halls, Harriett Stephens Wilson, Corrine Martin Ervin, Verda Miller Shields, and Frances Strait Brown must be remembered as the founders of Kitchen 8.

The *K8 Newsletter*, first published in 1988, is a great source of alumnae stories. I owe special thanks to Sarah Wohlrabe Shortall and Ali Bannwarth Zayas, editors of the more recent *K8 Newsletters* for their work. The Kitchen 8 historian, Laura Draxler Sixta, was key in having the hall scrapbooks scanned, so that they would never get lost or fade with time. Many of the hall scrapbooks are available online.

***Norma Decker Hoagland** (left), current president of Kitchen 8, and **Bev Runkle Benso** (right), Watkins Hall campus coordinator 2006–15.*

Watkins Museum of History has been a wonderful resource for this book, and Kitchen 8 owes a great thanks to the museum, our Watkins "cousin." We partner on many activities and they house the archives of Kitchen 8. Also, many documents and photos for this book are gratefully acknowledged from the University Archives at the Spencer Research Library at KU and the Kansas Historical Society.

My family has endured my enthusiasm and stories of Elizabeth for many years and I appreciate their support with this heartfelt work. I hope you enjoy reading about the life of these halls and what they have meant and still mean to so many young women.

— **Norma Decker Hoagland,**
Watkins Hall 1969–71

Photo Credits and Other Sources

Resident studying in the Watkins Hall living room, 2011

University Archives, Spencer Research Library, University of Kansas 4, 8 (left), 13, 14, 19, 27, 29, 31, 32, 34, 35, 40, 42, 43, 46, 47, 49, 52, 53, 54, 55

Watkins Museum of History 6, 7, 8 (right), 9, 10, 16, 17, 18, 21

Watkins Scholarship Hall 11, 36, 44, 45, 51, 57

Kansas Historical Society 12

First City Photo/Debra Bates-Lamborn 15, 33, 69

Kitchen 8 Archives, *Watkins Hall, Residence for Women,* 1926, printed by Kansas State Printing Plant, Topeka, Kansas 17, 20, 23 (upper), 24

Corrine Martin Ervin 22 (lower left), 30

Philomene Bourassa Hood, University of Kansas scrapbook, 1935, Elizabeth Miller Watkins Legacy Collection, Kansas Historical Society 22 (upper three and lower right), 25

Phillip and Paula Hopkins Wrigley: "A Plan of the Campus of the University of Kansas," Marjorie Whitney, 1926, (map preserved and passed down by Phillip's great-great-grandparents, Miles and Cara Sterling, 1883 graduates of KU) 23 (lower)

Miller Scholarship Hall 28 (upper), 50

Norma Decker Hoagland 28 (lower), 66 (left), 68, 72 (right)

Virginia Van Order Thomas 37

Marilyn Whiting Thomas 38, 39

Kitchen 8 Newsletters 41, 60, 61, 66 (right), 67 (upper left, right)

Kansas Alumni/Steve Puppe 56, 64, 70, 71

Judy Johnson Niebaum 58 (upper)

Carol Hemphill Starr 58 (lower)

Beverly Runkle Benso 59 (upper)

Lynne Lammers Coblammers 59 (lower)

Ali Bannwarth Zayas 62, 63

Gayle Barry Matchett 65

Laura Draxler Sixta 67 (lower left two)

John Clayton 72 (left)

Historic Mt. Oread Friends

Historic Mt. Oread Friends (HMOF), formerly Historic Mount Oread Fund, is pleased to have assisted with this publication. Beginning with *Old Fraser* in 1984, this is the fourth book in the series "Biography of a Building" that celebrates the history of the University of Kansas.

HMOF works to preserve and enhance the historic and beautiful KU campus. An all-volunteer nonprofit organization, HMOF was founded in 1981 through KU Endowment. We pool membership gifts to advance our mission through supporting campus preservation and beautification projects, as well as programming about KU history.

To learn more about HMOF or join, please contact:

historicmountoread.org
or
Historic Mt. Oread Friends
Kansas University Endowment Association
P.O. Box 928
Lawrence, Kansas 66044-9950

Other HMOF books:

Historic Mount Oread: A Catalog of KU's Landmarks, 1999
Old Fraser, 1984
Dyche Hall, 2003
Spooner Hall, 2009